This book belongs to:

_____

ISBN: 979-8-88759-352-4

Chachi's Storytime presents:

A Day of Joy
with
Daddi Ji

Spending the day with Daddi Ji is always a lot of fun.

As soon as she opens her door, her face shines as bright as the sun!

I run to her and say, "Hi Daddi Ji, I'm so excited to play!"

She walks me into the house and laughs,
"Aaj Apa Daddi-Pothi FUN Karan Gey!"

She always ties her Chunni around her head.
I try…but fail, so I'll look like a mummy and scare her instead!

We like to pick vegetables in the garden.
She says, "Tamatar," and I say, "Tomato".

She says, "Kheera," and I say, "Cucumber."
All these names are so much fun!

When I'm feeling naughty, I spray her with the hose.
I laugh and twirl and run away, and then I hear her groans!

Hai!

For all my furry friends, we host a tea party together.

She makes us Gulab Jamun, Jalebi, and Cha with love and pleasure.

We go to the playground to ride the swings, and she takes me in her arms to fly.

Up and up and up I go; never have I flown so high!

We have picnic lunches in the shade with Paratha and Achar—yummy!

She lets me eat until I have a very full tummy.

Daddi Ji proudly combs and oils my hair.
She ties it in a Guth like Princess Rapunzel wears.

She listens to Paaht, and together we pray.
This is the favorite part of my day.

Then comes the hard part when I must go.

I know she will miss me, and my love for her will grow.

She kisses me goodnight and hugs me very tightly.

"Don't worry, Daddi Ji...Main Dubara Tuhade Naal FUN Karan Avan Gi!"

www.ingramcontent.com/pod-product-compliance
Lightning Source LLC
LaVergne TN
LVHW072125070426
835511LV00003B/93

*9 7 9 8 8 8 7 5 9 3 5 2 4 *